Disclaimer

This book has been written to provide information about Internet marketing. Every effort has been made to make this book as complete and accurate as possible and this book provides information only up to the publishing date. Therefore, this book should be used as a guide - not as the ultimate source.

The purpose of this book is to educate. Glenda Boone, the author and the publisher, does not warrant that the information contained in this book is fully complete and shall not be responsible for any errors or omissions. Glenda Boone shall have neither liability nor responsibility to any person or entity with respect to any loss or damage caused or alleged to be caused directly or indirectly by this -book.

The Church Social Media Marketing Guide

Social media sites like Facebook and Twitter are the new trend of the internet. It opened new possibilities to communication and it improved the way people connect and share. Think of it as an online ground where people can meet and interact electronically.

But as you know, a church thrives where people thrive. And having realized the large number of people that login to social media sites on a daily basis, church pastors found a new marketing channel to grow their congregations using the internet and social media.

Today, social media sites are no longer just an ingenious way for people to meet, connect and share. It is now also one of the most powerful advertising tools which pastors can use to connect to their targeted market niche.

However, it is noteworthy that social media marketing is like a double-edged sword – it is something that needs to be wielded correctly. In the hands of a skilled marketer, it is an effective sales tool. But in the hands of an amateur, it can turn success into demise.

So to help you avoid the pitfalls of social media marketing, I made a list of 200 tips that will guide you to the proper use of social media sites. So read on and learn how your church can turn social media sites into an effective church marketing tool.

Tips on choosing which social media site to use

1. Choose a social media site that is popular in your area.

   Of course, you want people to view your social media site, especially your target market niche. However, there are social media sites that are popular in some countries but not in others.

   For instance, it appears that Facebook is more widely used in Asian countries while Western countries are more likely to be active on Twitter.

2. Consider using multiple social media sites.

   If you live in a place wherein there are several social media sites that are in use, perhaps you can sign up an account on all those social media sites. This way, you will be able to reach more people.

Tips on getting started with a social media site

3. Make a draft plan of the contents first.

   Getting started without a plan can lead to a messy start. This will not be good for your church's image. So before you make your social media account available, make sure that you planned for its contents and design first.

4. Come up with an editorial calendar.

You may have plenty of things you want to share and say. But if you post all of them at the same, people will get confused. Also, you will quickly run out of things to share in the future. So make a timeline and plan which things you want to post first and which ones should follow in a chronological order.

5. Know your target market niche.

    There are plenty of people that join social media sites. However, you do not really want to reach to all of them. You need to focus on a group of people which are 'potential e-church members'.

6. Check for a possibly existing account with a similar name.

    You do not want people to confuse your church for another organization, group, or individual. You do not know how these other accounts are behaving and anything they do might have implications on your churches image.

7. Try using checkusernames.com to create a unique moniker.

    If you found out that there are already existing accounts with a similar name or a mockingly similar name, you can go to checkusernames.com to help you come up with an alternative.

8. Know how to lure in the people in your target market niche.

   Do you already have a clear vision of who your target market niche is? The next thing you need to figure out is how you can lure them in. You need to conduct research on the things that interest them. For example, if your church focus is on community outreach, your market niche might be local politicians. If your target audience is less than 30 years of age your market niche would be millennials in your area.

9. Ready high quality graphics and Photoshop edited photos.

   Sometimes, it is not the content but the appearance. What really draws some people into a social media profile is the looks of it. You can make your profile page look more attractive by using pictures, photographs, and images.

10. Ready high quality short articles, comments, posts.

    After luring them in with flamboyant graphics and attractive page design, potential members will start looking for content. If they find nothing, they will leave. For some relevant content, you can hire people to write short articles, comments, and posts.

11. Make sure that you have the resources to regularly maintain a social media account.

    Yes, it is free to sign up to Facebook and Twitter. But you will need to hire graphics artists, video editors, content writers, and maintenance crew. And if you need to advertise, you will probably need to pay these social media sites. Make sure that you have a budget for it.

12. Check to see if having a social media account will really be of help to your church or if it will just be a liability.

    There are a lot benefits in having a social media account for your church. But there are also dangers. You need to analyze if you can take these risks head on.

13. Know the dangers and risks of having a social media account and see if it is worth it.

Tips on keeping subscribers glued to your account

14. Keep your pages looking beautiful and/or professional.

    You may need to hire people to do this for you. This is important because if your social media profile looks shabby, people will probably not have a very good impression of your church.

15. Sport a page design that corresponds to the nature of your church.

    You cannot just decide on what design to use based on your personal taste. Instead, it needs to be based on the nature of your services. For example, if your focus are for children, your page should look fun and colorful.

16. Regularly post new comments and news.

    If you do not post regularly, your subscribers will think that your church is not active and is slacking off. To avoid this, you need to post news and comments regularly.

17. Always respond to questions if possible. Avoid ignoring your subscribers.

    People will certainly ask questions. You should provide a response if you can. This is one way to show hospitality and people will appreciate it.

18. Do not always use just words. You can use multimedia once in a while.

    If all your announcements are just words and sentences, it will soon get boring no matter how interesting your posts are. So once in a while, try to convey what you want to say through videos, images, and presentations.

19. Try sporting several design schemes from time to time.

    One design theme throughout the year is too boring. It will also give people the impression that you lack resources, so try sporting a new look for your page from time to time. One good tip is to follow the changes of season (summer look, winter look) or you can also follow the coming of holidays (Christmas look, Halloween look).

20. Just a logo is not enough. Try uploading more photos related to your church.

Some churches only upload their logo. This is boring. You should post more photos about your church.

21. Always upload photos of recent events that involved your church.

    If your church recently hosted or attended an event, you should post photographs of it. This way, people will see that your church is active.

22. Do poll questions once in a while. Keep it exciting.

    Studies show that people like answering quick poll questions on social media sites. Try doing it once in a while to entertain your subscribers. But keep it related to your church. For example, if your pastor is preaching a sermon series, you can make a poll of which among the list of sermons was most impactful in their opinion.

23. Post updates about new promos that your church offers.

    Your social media profile is one good channel to announce promos and events that your church hosts. Also, it will keep your subscribers checking your profile.

Tips on using multimedia content

24. Use only high quality media content. Do not settle for mediocre quality.

    The quality of the media content you upload will have a huge impact on your church's image. Make sure that you only use high quality ones.

25. Instead of uploading videos to the actual social media account, considering using links instead.

    Some social media sites limit how many megabytes of file you can upload. So instead of uploading a video to the blog site, consider uploading them to Youtube first and link the Youtube URL to your blog site.

26. Choose multimedia designs that suit your targeted market niche.

    The design scheme of the multimedia contents you upload should match the nature of your church.

27. Always check for possible mistakes before uploading so as to maintain credibility.

    Especially if you hired people to make the video or graphics for you, it will be necessary that you check it for errors first before you upload it.

28. Know the upload limitations of your social media of choice.

    Facebook for example limits how many megabyte of file you can upload. Know these limits so you can plan how much multimedia file you can use to improve the look of your page.

29. Remove oldest multimedia uploads to free up your upload limit.

    If you ran out of storage space and you need to upload a new file, perhaps there are some previously uploaded media files that are no longer needed and may already be deleted.

30. Know which uploads should never be removed to matter what.

    Not all multimedia you previously uploaded may be removed. Some need to stay for your subscribers to see. For example, if you uploaded a video that features the products, you should probably keep that video file for new subscribers to see.

31. HD quality is good but do not always use it.

    Your subscribers will appreciate an HD quality video upload. But it will take a lot of space. Even if you use Youtube, an HD file will take longer to load on slower connections.

32. The dimension of photographs does not always have to be big in order to be high quality.

    There is this connotation that the higher the pixels, the better the quality and clarity. But it is not always the case. It all depends on the editing. A 640x480 photo may look clearer than a 1024x720 photo.

Tips on using language

33. Decide on a language to use.

    English is considered the international language. But there are still plenty of people who cannot understand English. If your target is a small locality, maybe you can use their language instead.

34. Consider duplicate pages that are translated to other languages.

    If you are targeting a market niche that is composed of people from different countries and ethnicities, perhaps you can make several accounts that use a specific language.

35. Use appropriate tone and language that suits your targeted market niche.

    For children's toys, you should sound fun. For fashion items, you should sound trendy. For serious stuff, you should sound corporate.

36. Be precise and brief in your message.

    People hate to read lengthy messages. Some of them are also busy. So keep you posts and comments brief and concise.

37. Always double check spelling and grammar before posting.

    Grammatical errors and typos can tarnish your church image. People will think that your posts are done in a hurry with no regard for quality.

Tips on using YouTube effectively

38. Decide on the appropriate comment sharing settings of your Youtube account.

    You can decide if you want to block other users from posting comments on your videos and on your profile page. Do this to prevent possibly derogative comments.

39. Decide on whether to use the 'Like' and 'Dislike' button or not.

    Dislikes have an effect on potential members. If you think you video will get a lot of dislikes, you can turn this option off.

40. Learn how to use related tags.

    If you want people to easily find your uploaded video on Youtube, you should use tags which people are likely to use when typing keywords in the search bar. For computer products for examples, tags like iPad, laptop, internet, Intel, and such should be used.

41. Check comments regularly.

    If you decided to allow comments, you should check them regularly so you can deal with derogative and damaging comments as soon as possible.

42. Use the 'delete comment' option sparingly.

    In Youtube, a comment is not completely removed. The username of the person who posted it will still be there and with a note "Deleted comment". People will wonder why you delete a comment. So use it sparingly.

43. Using courteous and well-informed replies instead of deleting.

    Instead of deleting, you can reply to derogative messages instead. But do not be rude. Simply defend in a very convincing and informed manner. Make sure that readers will side with you because of the way you answered.

44. Customize your page and use your logo for better credibility.

Using the church logo adds credibility. And customizing your page makes it look more authentic.

45. Upload only high quality videos.

    Videos do not have to be in HD to be high quality and clear. It just needs to be properly done and edited. All videos should be high quality because it will affect the image of your church.

46. Screen videos for possibly offensive elements.

    People on Youtube can be pretty harsh. Make sure that all videos you upload are free of potentially offensive contents.

47. Take time to learn the policies of Youtube.

    It is damaging to the reputation of your church if your account gets suspended. People will wonder why it happened. So take time to read Youtube's policies.

48. Update users about increase in subscribers.

    Others usually update about their first 1000, 5000, 10,000 and 100,000 subscribers. Make these updates so your subscribers can see that your page is moving forward.

Tips on how to expand the reach of your social media account

49. Advertise your social media account.

    The purpose of your social media account is to advertise. However, a social media account is an advertisement tool that also needs to be advertised. Tell people to visit your social media account.

50. Always include your social media URL to your other forms of advertisement.

    If you advertise on magazines, television, and radio, you need to make sure that your social media account is mentioned. A small note saying "Visit us on Facebook" should be sufficient.

51. Learn to use SEO techniques.

    When making posts and uploading articles to your blog site, make sure that they are made with SEO. This will make your social media account easier to find via search engines.

52. Contribute SEO articles to websites like www.ezinearticles.com.

    By contributing SEO articles to these sites, you are making your social media page easier to find on the internet.

53. Use a URL name that corresponds to the main keyword which best describes your service offering or your church.

    You can change how your URL appears. For example, if your church name is The Gathering, you can change your Facebook URL to www.facebook.com/thegathering

54. Get affiliated with other groups which are related to your market niche.

    By becoming affiliates of other groups that are related to your field, you are exposing your page to more potential viewers. For example, if you are selling cosmetics, church merchandise probably become affiliated with pages about religious marketing materials and products..

55. Use follow buttons

    These are buttons which you can post elsewhere on the internet. This way, users can like content you posted in your Facebook account actually logging in to Facebook or opening another window.

56. Use share/link buttons.

    Have affiliate sites to post a link that will direct users to your churches website. This is one reason why it is important to have many affiliates on the internet. It will help you have more echurch member subscribers.

57. Make use of the old school method called email marketing.

Yes, it is old. But it is still effective. Send potential leads an email that contains a link and/or follow button that will connect them to your church's website or facebook page.

58. Propose a guest post on established and influential blogs – the big names ideally.

    Ask other influential groups to allow you to make a post on their page. And on that post, make sure to include a link that will direct users to you're your churches website and or facebook page.

59. Your subscription buttons should be done via RSS.

    This allows users to see the latest updates on your church's blog page.

Tips on outsourcing work and task

60. Make sure the account holder you hire knows your ideals and standards.

    You may choose to hire a person to manage and maintain your social media sites. Make sure they know your standards. They should understand how you want to run things.

61. Have someone check the site throughout the day and night.

You do not know when a user might have posted something derogatory on your page. Therefore, it is important that you have someone check your social media pages from time to time to filter out such comments.

62. Set limits on how much they can change.

    People you hire to manage your church's social media pages should have limitations. There are things that they should not touch or change. Be clear in this.

63. Authorize different actions to different people if necessary.

    For better results, you can hire someone who manages events, promos, news, and such. You should also have a person for articles, videos, graphics, and page design.

64. You can hire people to do the graphics.

    Photoshop is not easy. If you need professional results, hire someone to do it for you.

65. You can hire people to do the videos.

    There are several videomaker software available out there. If you are not confident, do not attempt to make your own. It will only lead to low quality output.

66. You can hire people to do the short articles.

    This is now easy to find. hire competent ghost/copy writers to write and post articles and even eBooks for you.

Tips on dealing with trolling, defamation, and other derogatory comments from users

67. Check for possibly derogatory messages all the time.

    Check your page all the time, or at least have someone do it for you. You need to deal with negative comments as soon as possible before they affect the opinion of other subscribers.

68. Avoid the domino effect of negative comments.

    When one person makes a negative comment, it is possible that others will sympathize. Then it can become a string of negative comments form more users. End it before this happens. Delete the root cause.

69. Do not leave a serious question hanging unanswered for too long.

    Some questions, if unanswered, can lead users to doubt your church's credibility (e.g. the product I bought is lasted only a month, can I have it replaced?). Questions like this one should be answered immediately.

70. Maintain a professional tone when replying to possibly derogative comments.

    Sometimes, you need to answer derogatory questions to set things straight, so other users will know the truth. But when doing so, you should avoid being rudely defensive. You should always maintain a professional tone. Other users will see this and appreciate it.

71. Know which messages should be left unanswered. You do not need to respond to every question.

Tips on using Facebook

72. Open a group account, not a personal account.

    There are two types of account you can open on Facebook. For social media marketing, you should open a group account instead of a personal account. Its features are designed for marketing.

73. Get your first 25 likes.

    A group account will only have access to all its features once it already gathers 25 likes from other users.

74. Consider getting a paid advertisement service, my firm will be more than happy to assist you with affordable facebook and Instagram advertising, visit out website at www.tasteandseemarkeing.com for information

    Facebook also offers a tool that will make your page appear on the advertisement section of other Facebook users. You can also set this option to appear only on a select market niche (age filters, address filter, gender filter, etc.). But this is a paid feature.

75. Post things that your subscribers will feel like sharing.

If one of your subscribers shares a post from your page, it will be available in their profile page. This way, it will be exposed to everyone in the friend list of that person. This will extend the reach of your social media account.

76. Like pages or groups which are in some way connected to your market niche.

    By liking pages from other groups, you are exposing yourself to the subscribers of those pages.

77. Like pages or groups which are frequented by your target members.

    Go to pages which your target members might frequent. For example, if your target members are women, you might find them fashion pages. Like those pages and perhaps post a comment to those pages to help them find you.

78. Get help from people you know who also have Facebook accounts.

    The start is the difficult part. Ask people you know to like your page. You can also ask them to share the contents of your page. Their friends can also help out.

79. Include a photo album which shows the faces of your church staffs.

    Studies show that people trust online organizations more if they can see faces. If there is no face, it is as if the organization is hiding something.

80. Keep the photo albums organized according to event and date.

    People like to browse photos. But it is annoying if different photos are just mixed together. Make sure that you organize them in albums.

81. Advertise your Facebook account on your other social media account.

    If you have a Twitter account for example, post a Tweet inviting your followers to check out your Facebook page as well.

82. Use only one account.

    This is to prevent confusion. If your services and or products are not widely varied, consider getting only one Facebook account.

83. Use several accounts only if your church has varied sectors.

    For example, if your church sells different stuff (e.g. clothes, food, toys), you should probably have a separate account or separate page for each genre.

84. Use your Facebook account to connect with people you meet on business trips and meetings.

    If you met possible affiliates on meetings and business trips, you can use your church's Facebook account to stay connected with them.

85. Your Facebook posts should be in harmony with your Twitter posts, if you have both.

    Contradicting posts on your Twitter and Facebook account will be seen as an inconsistency. Subscribers might question how your church runs things.

86. Update users about increase in subscribers.

    Tell people that your number of subscribers is growing! This will give the impression that your church is moving forward.

Tips on using Twitter

87. Edit the URL name and use a main keyword which best describes your church.

    From the default URL assigned to your profile by Twitter, edit it into something like www.twitter.com/YouChurchNameHere.

88. Regularly post news and events.

    If you leave your Twitter account unattended, people will stop following you. And even if they do not unfollow you, they might stop checking your posts.

89. Follow groups, organizations, companies, and/or people which you believe are connected to your church in some way.

Follow twitter accounts that are related to the nature of your business. This will increase your exposure to more Twitter users.

90. Avoid posting Tweets on other's profile.

    This is to maintain a professional attitude. Remember, this is a church account not a personal account.

91. Avoid using your church Twitter account for personal business.

    If you like a certain celebrity or you like to make comments about some current events that are completely unrelated to your business, you should follow them using your own personal account. Business and personal life should not be mixed together.

92. Avoid conveying personal feelings and thoughts via your church's Twitter account.

    Tweets about your bath time, the breakfast you had, the new clothes you bought, and your quarrel with your friends do not belong in your church Twitter.

93. Advertise your Twitter account on your other Social media account.

    If you have a Facebook account, tell your Facebook subscribers that you also have a Twitter account. This way, both your accounts will show more subscribers.

94. Hashtags are not very effective.

    If you like doing this trick, well save it. A recent study shows that posts that used hashtags are actually 5% less efficient at attracting users.

95. Do not follow more people than the number of people following you.

    If you are following more people than the number of people of following you, it will make you look desperate. This is not good for your church's image. You must exercise some degree of self-importance.

96. Use geo-location to find local target niche.

    This feature is very useful for internet marketing. It will help you locate your target members better.

97. Focus more on your advocates than your influencers.

    You influencers are only likely to mention you once or twice. After which, you are not really connected with them. But advocates are different. They are potentially long term members with long term benefits. Invest time on them.

98. Your Tweets should be in harmony with your Facebook posts, if you have both.

    Make sure that church news, events, and promos you Tweet are the same with those you post on your Facebook account.

99. Update users about increase in followers.

Tips for safety

100. Be transparent while exercising caution.

    Your subscribers will like it if you are transparent. They will feel connected with you. But you must limit how much information you withhold.

101. Only withhold the physical address or office address of the church itself.

    You are not obliged nor is it safe to tell your subscribers your personal address or the personal address of your employees. Only tell them the address of the church itself.

102. Only withhold the church contact number, email, fax, etc.

    Only the church contact information should be advertised. Those of the employees should not be disclosed to protect their privacy.

103. Avoid heated conversation.

    Not only is it unprofessional, but it will not leave a good impression on your subscribers.

104. Keep a record of possibly threatening comments from users.

    If a post includes threats or anything of the same degree, you should keep a record of it. A printscreen will do.

105. Never use a password that is easy to guess.

    You do not know what hackers might do to your account. Make sure that your password is something that cannot be guessed.

106. Never withhold the email address that is used to register the social media account.

    This may all be that a hacker needs to hack into a Facebook or a Twitter account. It should be kept private.

107. Use a registration email that is different from the church's email.

    A hacker will normally attempt to use the official church email thinking that it is used to open your church's Facebook or Twitter account.

108. Never leave the account unattended in any computer.

109. Do not forget to uncheck the 'Keep Me logged' in button.

    Some people forget to uncheck this box. As a result, their account gets hacked by the next person who will use the computer. Good thing if it is found by a good person.

110. Avoid logging in to public computers.

    Even if you uncheck the Keep Me Logged in button, there still ways for hackers to get your username and password. A simple keylogger program will do the trick.

111. If you must login using a public computer or a public network, try using the onscreen QWERTY board when keying in the username and password.

    Keylogger programs follow the keystrokes that you make. They cannot read passwords and usernames that are inputted using an onscreen qwerty keyboard. The downside is that people behind you will see which characters you clicked.

112. Change the password if you believe it has been compromised.

113. Remove arguments between users.

    Sometimes, the dispute may not be between you and a user but amongst users themselves. Remove these as soon as possible. Block them if necessary.

114. Set a rules and conditions page.

    Some people may not exactly follow. But if you ban them, they will not be able to say that they were not warned.

Tips on involvements you should avoid

115. Avoid 'liking', 'following' or getting linked in any way to celebrities.

    This is part of professionalism. Business is business and involvement with Hollywood seems like a personal thing to do unless the celebrity you will feature is somehow linked to your business.

116. Avoid 'liking', 'following' or getting linked in any way to politicians.

    People are always divided in their political views. You could lose possible members if you favor politicians and political decisions which they do not approve of.

117. Avoid voicing opinions on controversial matters.

    Other than politics, there are other events that can divide the opinion of people. Avoid making statements about such matters.

118. Avoid using your church's social media account to post comments that convey your personal feelings and thoughts.

    You may have opinions about current events. But you should avoid making them on your church's social media account.

119. Avoid uploading contents that are not related to your market, unless it is part of your marketing strategy.

Sometimes, it might be necessary to add some fun stuff as a form of entertainment. But do not make it a hobby.

120. Avoid media contents which are potentially offensive to any group or people.

    Racism is especially a sensitive topic. Avoid making any comment, even a commercial joke, because people are not likely to take it lightly.

121. Avoid jokes, unless they are completely inoffensive.

Tips on maintaining/improving the credibility of your social media account

122. If your church has an official webpage, make sure to mention your social media account in your official webpage.

    This is one way of encouraging people to subscribe to your social media account. If you get them to subscribe to you, you are also gaining access to the people in their friend list.

123. Do forget to use your church logo in your social media account.

124. Post photos of church events – the kinds which the public could not possibly have had access to.

    Random photos like dinners, tours, and even photos in airports are the kinds of photos that others could not have access to. This way, people will know that your social media account is authentic and is the real thing.

125. Make sure your social media announcements correspond to the announcements your official webpage.

    If you are also making announcements on your official webpage, they should be the same with the details of the announcements you make on your social media account.

126. Be careful about making statements about current events. Avoid it if possible.

    People have different opinions about current events. If you favor one side, you might incite the anger of some people.

127. Always give your subscribers the feeling that the church is moving forward.

    People will like you more if they believe that your church is moving forward. Always give this impression through the posts that you make.

128. Always give your subscribers the feeling that your church's social media account page is active and kicking.

129. When mistakes happen, step up and own the mistake.

    Even with a lot of precaution, it is possible that a mistake or two could slip up. When this happens, just admit it and apologize.

People will appreciate this better. They will see through a denial and will hate it.

130. Act like a leader, without being cocky.

    People need to feel that you are a leader – a driving force. IF you do this without being cocky, they will respect you.

131. Always post media exposure of your church.

    If your church has been featured in a magazine, a television show, or any media channel, make sure that you mention it on your social media site. Provide a link if available.

Tips on measuring and improving the effectiveness of your social media account

132. Analyze how many of your members came to you through your social media account.

    Run polls and surveys to know how many of your members learned about your church through your social media account. This way, you will know if your social media venture is fruitful or not.

133. Blog regularly for better traffic.

    Making blog posts on a regular basis will keep people tuned in to your page. It will increase traffic. After all, they will not regularly check a page that rarely makes blog posts.

134. Imagine that social media is like a story that you tell, and the characters in the story are your members.

135. Do not always just talk about your church. Talk about the people that subscribe to you.

    If you speak about you subscribers and members as well, they will feel that they are important and that they are involved. This will improve your relationship with them.

136. Use polls so you learn more about your members.

    Polls let you know the preferences of your subscribers. This will give you an idea about your next marketing plans.

137. Try other smaller scale social media sites for localized marketing.

    If there is a local social media site in the area of your targeted market niche, consider opening an account there as well. This is to help you reach to more locals.

138. Offer a mobile check-in feature if it is compatible with your church.

    It is now getting popular that churches allow their members to order and/or check-in for services and/or products online. Offer this feature to open up to more e-members.

Tips on coming up with a good content

139. Always stay updated about current events.

    Current events may give you ideas about the future of your market. Stay updated so you are not left behind in market changes.

140. Check the latest news in your field.

    You need to check for current events but you need to focus more on news that involve your market niche. You can also make posts about these news events as long as you do not side with any group.

141. Regularly check yahoo news.

    The homepage of yahoo is one of the great places to find some of the juiciest and latest news. They also often feature business news.

142. Regularly read magazines that are related to your field.

    Magazines can give you a lot of ideas.

143. Hire researchers if possible.

    Research is not an easy task, especially if it involves marketing and business. If you do not have the extra time for it, you can hire people to do it for you.

144. Think out of the box and come up with something unique.

Try going out of your comfort zones once in a while. Think of new exciting ways to make your announcements and posts so that your subscribers are not bored.

145. If you need to recycle content, make sure it is redone from the bottom up.

    Sometimes, you just really run out of a fresh new content. While recycling is discouraged, sometimes it is the only thing that could save you. But if you must do this, make sure that you make it look new and different.

146. Ask your membeers and subscribers what they want to see next.

    IF you have no idea what your subscribers might like to see next, you can simplify things by asking them straight ahead. In fact, members like it when you ask questions like: "What do you want to see next?"

147. Ask your member influencers what they want you to do next.

    Do not just ask your members and subscribers. You should not forget about your affiliates, advocates, and influencers as well. Ask them.

148. Check your previous contents and check out what might be missing.

    You might think that you have already done almost everything. But check your profile again. You never know what you might discover that is missing.

Tips on writing your comments and posts effectively

149. Come up with a good title.

    Sometimes, subscribers will not even try to read if they see that a post is lengthy. So what should you do? Incite their interest by starting your post with a catchy and intriguing title.

150. Always use a catchy headline.

    If a title is inappropriate, then simply start the sentence with a catchy and interesting first sentence.

151. Use the inverted triangle method of writing.

    In article writing, this means that you should write your articles by including all the important information in the beginning of the article. The concentration of information is higher in the beginning and gets fewer as the article ends.

Tips on unique ways to deliver your message

152. Use PowerPoint presentations.

    Tired of old-school paragraph posts? Then create a powerful presentation instead and add some exciting designs and animations.

153. Use images.

    You can also make a graphic art of what you want to say.

154. Use video clips.

    This is just like doing a PowerPoint presentation.

155. Use voice clips.

    Try something new once in a while and convey your message through a recorded voice. This is actually a more effective marketing strategy because a voice can be more encouraging than written words.

156. Combine all of the above.

    All the tricks used above can be used at the same time. This will make for a unique and effective way of communicating with your subscribers.

157. Use lists and bullet points.

    A long paragraph is tiring to read. Make it easier for your subscribers to read by making a list instead.

158. Use uppercase letters on important words.

    This is one way to entice your subscribers to read a rather boring- looking paragraph. Highlight words like BONUS, SALE, PROMO, and such. Seeing keywords like these ones will surely catch their attention.

159. Use double quotations as necessary.

    Other than CAPSLOCK, this is another effective way to highlight an important word.

160. Use underlines as necessary.

    Underlines are also an effective highlighting element.

161. Use highlighting if your social media blog allows this feature.

    Adding a colored highlight to a word will probably make it stand out more than a capslock, a double quote, or an underline can. Sadly, not all social media sites offer the option.

162. Know the proper use of the opening word "ATTENTION!"

    Sometimes, you can simply start a paragraph with "ATTENTION!". Use this sparingly. And make sure that the message is really worth the opening.

163. An occasional humor is okay.

Professionalism should be observed at all times but some humor will put a smile on the face of your readers. If they are happy, they are more likely to buy.

164. Subscribe to newsletters of influencers.

165. Subscribe to newsletters of similar groups

166. Subscribe to newsletters of competitors.

Tips on improving customer relationships

167. Write about success stories of your members.

    Feature examples of some of your members or visitors who liked your service and/or product. This will invite others to avail of your product/service as well.

168. Post how-to guides for your subscribers.

    It has been proven in internet marketing that most internet users like reading how-to-guides. If you always provide some once in a while, people will keep coming back to check your page.

169. Include guides about things to avoid.

    This way, your members and subscribers will feel that you actually care about their well-being. This will be good for your church.

170. Post interviews with a successful member

Do not just tell stories about a successful member. Instead, you should probably post a video of an interview. This is a lot more convincing that just plain text.

171. Avoid recycling previous messages.

    You may have no choice but to recycle content in some instances. But avoid it if at all possible. Some users will still notice that a content is recycled even after a lot of editing and changes.

172. Avoid recycling multimedia elements.

    Not just words and articles, but multimedia content may also be recycled. But do so only when you have no choice. Also, you should edit it so that it is not recognizable as a recycled item.

173. Send out important newsletters to subscribers.

    Sometimes, subscribers just stop checking out your page and it is not even your fault. Maybe they just got busy for a period of time and forgot. In which case, it helps to remind them through newsletters.

174. Always use courteous greetings, daily if possible.

    On days when you have nothing to say, perhaps a simple "Good morning" and "Good evening" or "Happy lunch time" will do. You may also use greetings as an opening to any announcement. Your subscribers will like a courteous attitude.

175. Make sure your subscribers feel that they are always up-to-date.

    This is one of the advantages of making announcements and news regularly. Our subscribers will feel that they are not left out of the latest about your church.

176. Talk about latest trends which you know your members will like and love to hear about.

Tips on dealing with competition

177. Check the social media site of your competitor.

    Who knows? Your competitor might have come up with a cool new idea to present ideas. Looking at the page of your competitor will give you more ideas which you can use together with your own original ideas.

178. Check the official homepage of your competitor.

    You can also take a look at the official webpage of your competitor to check out how they advertised their social media account.

179. Subscribe to the newsletter of your competitor.

    You can use your personal account for this. You can subscribe to the newsletters of your competitors to see what they are up to. This may also give you new ideas for your marketing strategies.

180. Avoid making negative statements about your competitor.

    Some may do this to demerit their competitors. But this is a dirty trick which many of your subscribers will recognize and hate. It will not be good for your image.

181. If your competitor posts anything against you, avoid getting lured into the trap answering back.

    A simple defense on your part to clarify false accusations will do. But do not return the favor of insulting back. If you do, you will appear as the good guy and your competitor will appear as the bad guy. People will also like how you just let it slide.

182. Avoid having things that are mockingly similar to that of your competitor.

    You check your competitors for ideas. But do not copy what their ideas. Do not post anything similar or use any idea that is exactly the same. At least, make some changes to it and make it your own.

183. Always be a step ahead.

    You cannot always be just copying ideas from your competitors. Instead, you have to take the lead. You have to be the trendsetter.

184. Check the number of hits your competitor's have.

    This will let you know how well your competitor is doing compared to your performance. This will tell you if you need to improve your performance more.

Tips on financing your social media account

185. Some social media only needs to be checked once a day.

    Checking once daily may be all that your social media account needs. IF this is the case, there is no need to pay an extra just to have it checked several times a day.

186. Check your database for currently existing multimedia content.

    Maybe there is no need to order new logo or graphics. Check the ones you used in your previous videos and slideshows. Maybe you can still use some of them.

187. Supply currently existing graphics to hired multimedia artists.

    It might help cut the cost if you provide artists you hire with currently existing graphics and logo.

188. Hire freelancers to do tasks.

    Instead of hiring a regular employee, it is better to hire a freelancer to do the job. It is less costly. You can use micro outsourcing sites like www.tasteandseemarketing.com.

189. Freelancers from Asian countries are usually cheaper to hire.

    Asian freelancers are not necessarily less competent. In fact, many of them produce world class quality. But because of their location, their asking price is lower.

190. Use safe payment methods.

    There is no need to expose your credit card number or your bank account number. There is also no need to expose your physical address by sending money via a courier. Instead, you can use safe payment methods like Paypal which protects your personal and account information.

191. Check if there is someone among your employees who can do the task.

    Maybe there is really no need to hire another person to do the task. Ask your employees. Maybe some of them have the skills to make multimedia content and write articles for your social media page.

192. Check if financing your social media site is getting returns.

    Maintaining a social media site might cost money and time. If it is not yielding you results, maybe it is not an effective marketing strategy for your line of business.

Tips on making your social media account user friendly

193. Tell the designer to use a page design that works well on smartphones.

    Many people check and update their social media accounts regularly via their smartphones. So it will help if your blog page is optimized for smartphone viewing.

194. Avoid using scripts and content that might run only on the latest software.

    Some multimedia content require the latest plugins. Such multimedia contents might now be viewable to all people. So avoid using the most latest ones.

195. Avoid making a page that might upload too slowly.

    You need a good page design. However, your page designer must avoid using elements that might take time to load. Now all viewers have a good internet connection and some will not wait for a page that loads too slowly.

196. Keep things looking neat.

    It does not have to be the most stylish. What is important is that your page looks clean – nothing is out of place.

197. Keep the information organized.

Elements and contents should be arranged and grouped properly. You should make it in a way that your subscribers will find things easily.

198. Use tabs (if possible) or divisions for different topics.

This will allow you to separate different topics and/or discussions. It will help keep your contents organized without opening multiple social media accounts.

199. Avoid high-falutin words.

Just keep it simple. Research shows that most internet users hate high-falutin words and they prefer a simple content.

200. Make your page easy to find.

There are many ways to do this. Using SEO and having plenty of backlinks for example will make your page easier to find on the internet. You can hire an internet marketing specialist to do this for you.

Conclusion

And this concludes my list of 200 tips for effective social media marketing. But of course, you should not just religiously stick to these rules. Be sensitive to the changes you see and act accordingly.

Be aware of the dangers of social media sites. Take note that many lives have been ruined because of Facebook and Twitter. Of course, these sites are not to be blamed. These things happen because of improper use of these social media sites.

So if you want to use Facebook, Twitter, and other social media sites to your advantage, you need to master its ways. You can start by learning about the pitfalls and learning how to avoid them.

Glenda Boone

www.ingramcontent.com/pod-product-compliance
Lightning Source LLC
Chambersburg PA
CBHW050028230526
45470CB00003B/1180